THE SERIOUS GUITARIST

LEFT-HAND TECHNIQUES

A skill-building approach for the dedicated guitarist

Mark Burgess

Alfred Music
P.O. Box 10003
Van Nuys, CA 91410-0003
alfred.com

ISBN-10: 1-4706-1661-0 (Book & CD)
ISBN-13: 978-1-4706-1661-8 (Book & CD)

Cover and interior photographs by Larry Lytle.

Alfred Cares. Contents printed on environmentally responsible paper.

CONTENTS

INTRODUCTION

The purpose of this book is to give the serious student of the guitar sets of exercises specifically designed to benefit the form and function of the left hand. It is meant to be a companion to my first book, *The Serious Guitarist: Right-Hand Picking* (Alfred #40913). Here, we will focus primarily on left-hand dexterity and technique, with exercises culled directly from my three decades plus of guitar experience—both as a student and as a professional guitarist. Included are the exercises that I've found to be most effective, the ones I've gotten the most out of through the years.

As with *Right-Hand Picking,* our focus will be on *how* to play, not *what* to play. If your technique is sound, and the hands are prepared to execute whatever combination of notes the music requires, then all you have to do is play them. There is no need to change your technique to play certain things. You can, but it's better to do something with intent, as a conscious choice, than attempt to accidentally stumble upon a way to play a certain piece of music. We will be focusing on getting the left hand prepared for any musical challenge. Then, whatever music is in your head can be brought out through your hands and into the world.

Many of the major concepts introduced here were adopted from the Guitar Craft courses I attended over a period of years. These courses had a profound influence on my playing, as well as continuously informing my life. Robert Fripp, Curt Golden, Tony Geballe, and many others who were present at the various courses I attended are owed a debt of gratitude that can never be fully repaid.

Thank you to Donny Trieu, Burgess Speed, Jared Meeker, Daniel Cohan, Link Harnsberger, Ron Manus, and everyone at Alfred Music for making this book possible. And, as always, my gratitude and admiration to Robert Fripp for his inspiration and guidance.

–Mark Burgess

About the CD

The included CD features audio recordings of the exercises in this book. Listening to the recordings will help you accurately interpret the feel and rhythm of each exercise. Look for the icon to the left, along with its corresponding track number, as you progress through the book.

A Few Words About Practice

Practice is, generally speaking, a fairly misunderstood concept. When we sit down with our instrument, whether it be a guitar or another instrument, we want to sound good. We want to play music that appeals to us and anyone else who may be in the range of hearing. But, that is not practice—that is playing, and there is a very big difference between the two.

Practice is about moving slowly toward a goal. It is about incremental changes that, over time, become transformative. Of course, the problem is, practice is hard and can be frustrating. It takes time. More specifically, it takes sustained effort over time. What this means is you need to use your time wisely. If you play an exercise that is very easy for you, move on. If you play (or attempt to play) an exercise that is very difficult, that is where you should spend your time. That area of weakness is what true practicing is for, to address a specific problem and eliminate it. When it's gone, it'll never be a problem again.

Breaking down a piece of music (or exercise) into small chunks is a very effective way to correct problems. Try reducing a piece of music down to a few notes or a single passage. It's often one single spot, or motion, that we miss consistently that needs to be fixed in order to play something accurately. Until that single problem is fixed, we will continue to stumble at that spot.

Twenty minutes of focused practice is better that two hours of noodling in front of the television (a habit we're often guilty of, make no mistake). Get into a routine. Practice at a certain time of day, for a certain amount of time. Cultivate a habit of focused and effective practice, and you will make progress quickly.

We all have busy schedules, so it may be difficult to make the time to practice. But, you have to make the time to get better as a guitar player. And, remember, by "practice," we mean practice—not play. Of course, playing is very important, too. After all, we play the guitar in the first place because it's fun. It's very satisfying to be able to play, so you should "play guitar" every day. But getting to the next level of musicianship, whatever that may be for you, will require genuine practice.

The Rabbit Hole

We do want to remind serious guitar students that it can be easy to get carried away with practicing and with exercises. The exercises presented in this book are proven to be effective, having a very specific and measurable impact. Some are infinite in their variations, so we heartily encourage you to explore them within what is reasonable for you. But let's also remember to not spend too much time with only exercises—go out there and play as well!

LEFT-HAND CONCEPTS

Making It Musical

Exploring variations can be very useful, especially if you are addressing a specific shortcoming in your playing. The Make It Musical examples in this book help show how to use the exercises in normal playing, as well as creating music. When you play an exercise, try thinking of it as a musical passage, and it will be. Even exercises that are dissonant or atonal on the surface often yield very usable and musical ideas in a different context. Try adding an effect (like distortion or delay), displacing a phrase rhythmically or intervallically, changing a rhythm or time signature, and you may find yourself with a unique, interesting musical idea. It is important to realize that exercises are a means to an end, and not an end in themselves. The ultimate goal is to play better guitar and become a better musician.

The Nomenclature of the Numbers

Throughout this book, we refer to "up" and "down," and "higher" and "lower," when referencing the exercises and how to play them. In each case, we are referring to musical, not physical, direction. The strings of the guitar are traditionally numbered from 1, the thinnest and highest in pitch (and closest to the floor), to 6, the thickest and lowest in pitch. The frets are numbered from 1, closest to the nut, up to however many are available on your guitar.

Left-Hand Position

Proper left-hand position begins and ends with relaxation. Begin from a sitting position, which is how most of us practice. Let the arm hang down to your side, face the palm of your left hand forward, and bring your hand to the neck of the guitar. It is important that you bring your hand to the guitar, and not the guitar to your hand. Many players will "grab" the neck of their guitar and move it, then hold it in place with their left hand. This places a tremendous amount of undue strain on the left hand. All that tension is translated into immobility and fatigue.

The guitar should be at a slightly upward angle so that the headstock is at shoulder level, especially when sitting. Try having the guitar at the same level when you're sitting or standing. This way, you will not have to change your position when you stand up. The guitar should be roughly perpendicular to your torso (from your line of sight), so that the headstock is just in front of the left shoulder. Now, bring your hand to the neck and place the pad of your thumb pointing straight up in the middle of the back of the neck, between the 2nd and 3rd fingers.

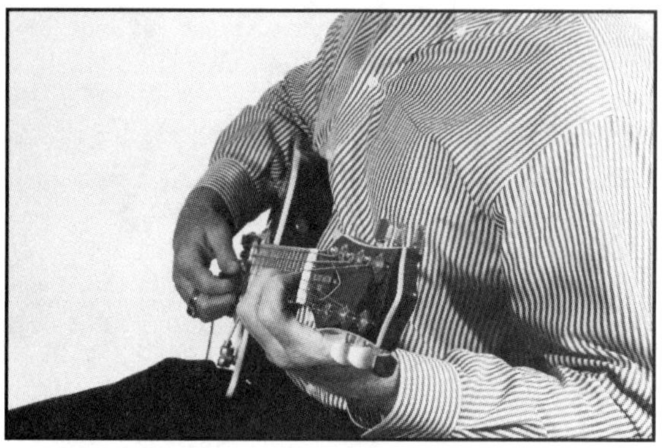

Guitar should be perpendicular to your torso with the headstock in front of your left shoulder.

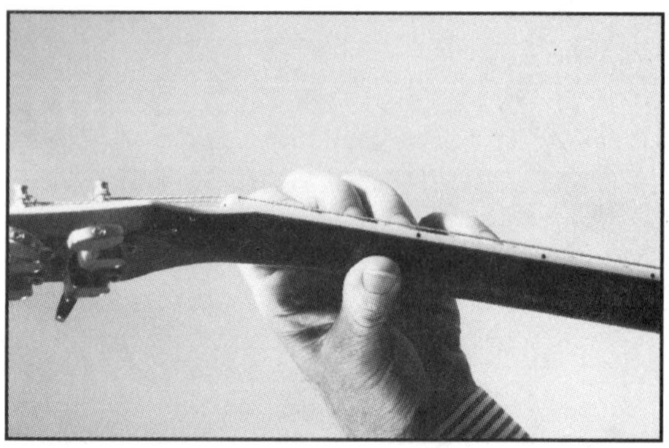

Pad of thumb in the middle of the neck, between the 2nd and 3rd fingers.

A common mistake is to wrap your thumb around the top of the neck. But with the thumb down (see photos on page 6), the hand and fingers will be free to move in any direction needed, up or down the neck or strings. There is no rule to say exactly where the thumb should be 100 percent of the time, but the following description of hand position at the first four frets is a good place to start. Curve your fingers gently around the bottom of the neck, and float them about 0.5″ to 0.75″ above the fretboard, between the 3rd and 4th strings. The tips of the fingers should be on the same plane, forming a straight line. The 1st finger should be just below (that is to say on the nut side) of the 1st fret. The 2nd finger should be just below the 2nd fret. The 3rd and 4th fingers are under the 3rd and 4th frets respectively.

At this point, the only part of the left hand touching the guitar is the pad of your left thumb. This is the *position of readiness* (which is a Guitar Craft idiom I've adopted). The hand is relaxed, ready to play, and able to move in any direction called for by whatever music you wish to play. Now, we are ready to actually play notes.

When playing single notes on the guitar, only the tips of the fingers and the pad of the thumb are in contact with the neck. Having the fingers curved with the hand in front of the neck allows you to engage the larger muscles of the hand, as well as the smaller muscles of the fingers. When playing chords or bending notes, it is often necessary to move the thumb to the top of the neck for support to generate the force needed for bends or playing multiple strings. However, when practicing the majority of the exercises in this book, the idea is to keep the thumb down so that the left hand can stay nimble, mobile, and above all, relaxed. The idea is to apply the proper amount of force necessary and no more. Apply it at the proper place at the proper time, with nothing wasted.

Pressure and Release

Let's dig into the concept of *pressure and release.* In the previous sections, we've discussed the fingers and how they should, when not playing actual notes, float in a straight line approximately 0.5″ to 0.75″ above the fretboard. In order for this to happen, it helps if you think of the fingers as "applying" and "releasing" pressure, as opposed to "putting down" and "lifting up" your fingers. This helps minimize effort and makes the working of the fingers more efficient. When you play a note, apply only the pressure necessary to get the note to sound cleanly. When you're ready to play a different note, the finger should simply release the pressure and it will come off the fretboard by itself. There is no need to "lift" it. In fact, what lifting does is cause the fingers not being employed to end up much farther away from the fretboard–and more distance means more effort in the long run.

The Principle of Simultaneous Release

The *principle of simultaneous release* refers to the practice of leaving the fingers on the fretboard after they have been placed there until a release is employed, at which time all the employed fingers are released. For example, the 1st finger is placed on the fretboard, and when a subsequent finger is placed on a higher fret, the finger on the lower fret remains. If another finger is placed above on a higher fret, the two lower fingers remain on the fretboard. When a finger on a lower fret is played, all the fingers above it release at the same time.

In the first variation of Exercise 1 (1–2–3–4, see page 9), the fingers are placed on the neck in ascending order: 1, then 2, then 3, then 4. Finger 1 should remain on the neck as finger 2 is placed. Then, fingers 1 and 2 remain while finger 3 is placed. Then fingers 1, 2, and 3 remain while finger 4 is placed. So now all 4 fingers of the left hand are on the fretboard. They should all release at the same time to move to another string or position. In the second variation (1–2–4–3), start with finger 1. Finger 1 remains as finger 2 is placed. Fingers 1 and 2 remain as finger 4 is placed, then those three fingers release simultaneously as finger 3 is placed. Check out the photos below for another variation.

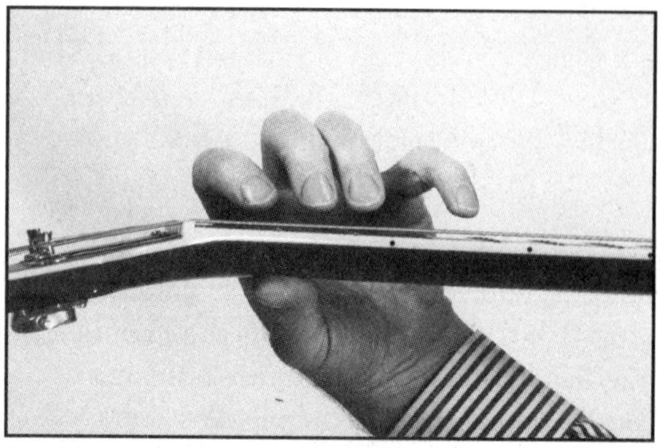

Position of readiness.

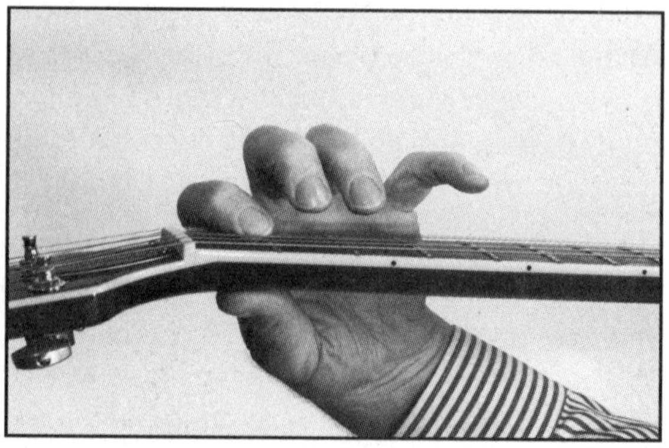

One finger down.

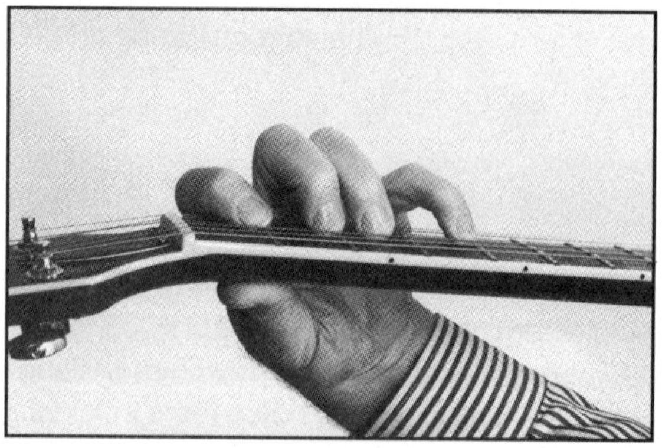

Four fingers down.

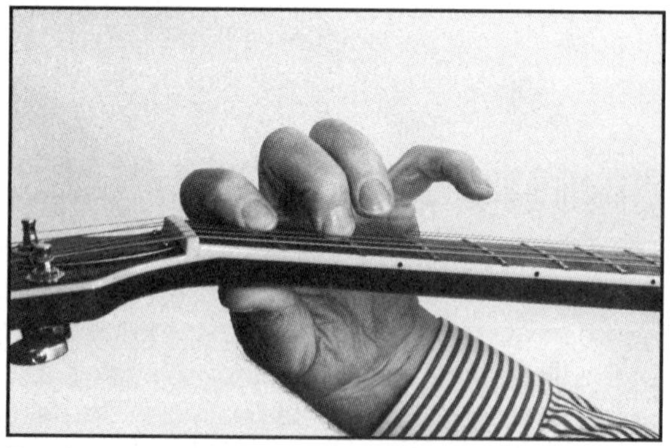

Two fingers down.

This technique can be a little tricky to get your head around at first, but practice slowly, and in a surprisingly short period of time, it will become second nature. Mastering this concept is essential to good left-hand technique, as it requires the fingers to remain in contact with the neck instead of floating out in space. It keeps your hand constantly in position, thereby promoting greater accuracy. It reinforces the economy of motion principle (that we covered in *The Serious Guitarist: Right-Hand Picking*) by helping eliminate unnecessary movement, and thus improving the accuracy of the left hand.

Using a Metronome

It is imperative to use a metronome when working through the exercises in this book. You can purchase a metronome at any local music store for less than ten dollars. There are online metronomes (http://webmetronome.com) and metronome applications that can be downloaded to your computer or smart device. A metronome will not only help you develop an accurate sense of time, it will also serve as a record of your progress. Keeping track of the settings at which you are able to maintain clean, accurate picking allows you to see your playing improve over time.

There are several strategies to take with a metronome, most involving the subdivision of the beat. Begin at what may seem a ridiculously slow tempo, such as ♩ = 48. Play through the exercise as it's written. Then play the rhythms as triplets. This allows you to speed up the exercise without stopping to adjust the tempo. Next, double the tempo by dividing all the written note values in half. If possible, repeat the previous two steps. If that's too fast, an adjustment to the metronome is needed. With this method, you can play any given exercise at five different tempos without ever having to adjust the metronome.

Working at these very slow tempos has another advantage. Instead of having the metronome play a click every time you are supposed to play a note, you are required to fill the space between the clicks evenly, as the beats get divided. You could even decrease the tempo more, so the metronome is playing only beats 1 and 3, or only on beat 1. That will help you develop an even more accurate sense of time as you would be responsible for accurately playing more of each measure on your own.

When it's time to increase the tempo, you can go up two settings, or clicks. These will represent different increments of time depending on the metronome you have. Moving up two clicks usually results in a setting that is a little too fast. That's OK. Work there for a while. If you are able to maintain right hand integrity, great. You've increased your playing tempo by 2 bpm (beats per minute). If not, back the tempo down one click, and you should be able to play the exercise there. In that case, you've increased your effective playing tempo by one click instead of two, but you're still a bit faster than you were before. Remember that you are striving for clean, accurate picking where all the notes are even and clear. Increasing the tempo more than three or four clicks in a week is very unusual, so be patient. Go slow. Nothing really good happens quickly.

Before we move on to the next section, practice the exercises below to get acquainted with working with the metronome in this new way.

⊓ = Downstroke
V = Upstroke

Metronome Exercise 1

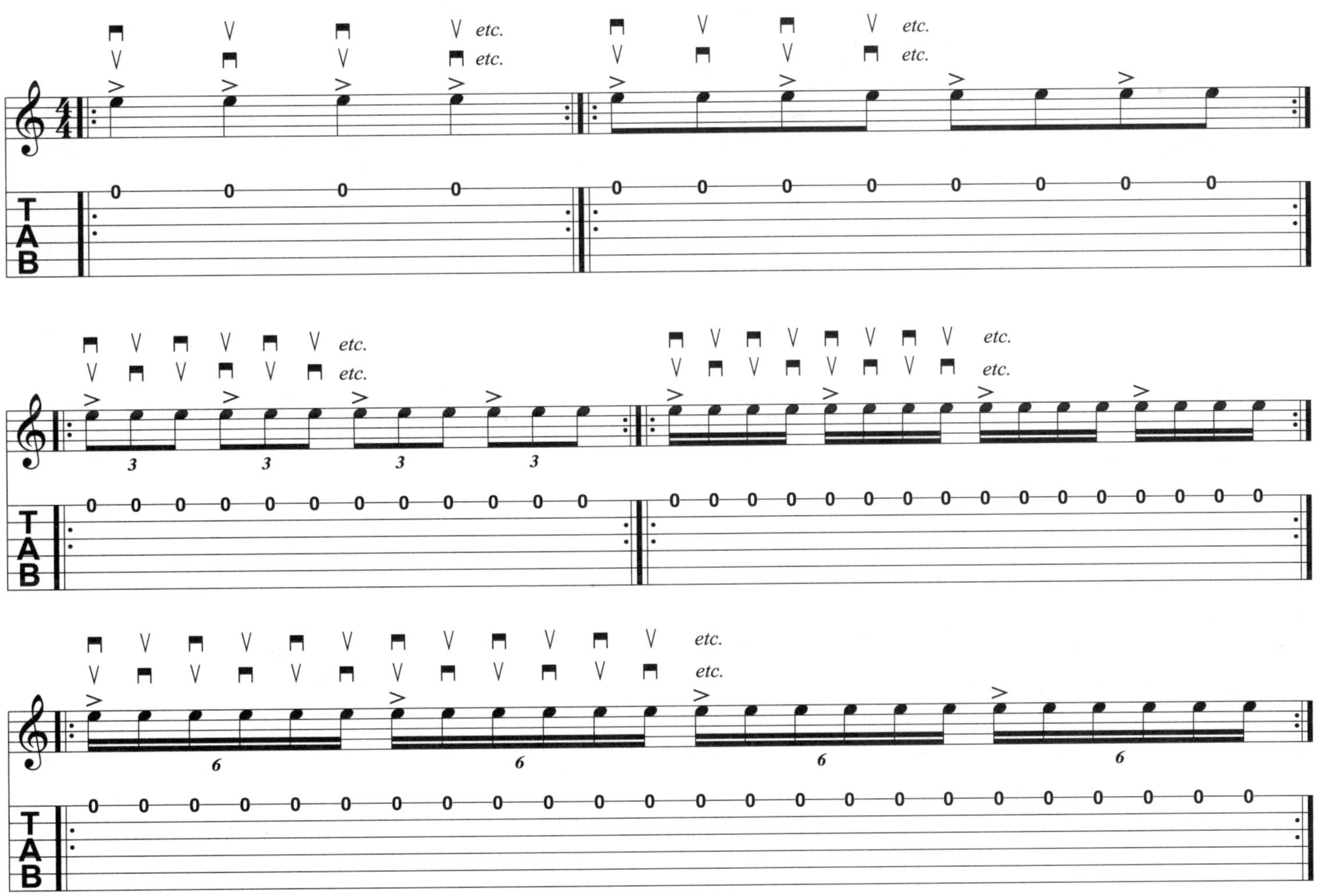

CHROMATIC EXERCISES

The first exercise presented is a basic "chromatic" four-finger exercise. It moves from the 6th string to the 1st string in 1st position, then shifts up one fret, and uses the same pattern to come back from the 1st to the 6th string. Shift up one fret, and start again.

Often, there are certain variations that will prove to be more difficult than others—these are the ones to work on. A metronome will always be an invaluable tool for keeping the time steady, as well as allow you to measure your progress. Play Exercise 1 using alternate picking.

Exercise 1—Chromatic Four-Finger Exercise 2

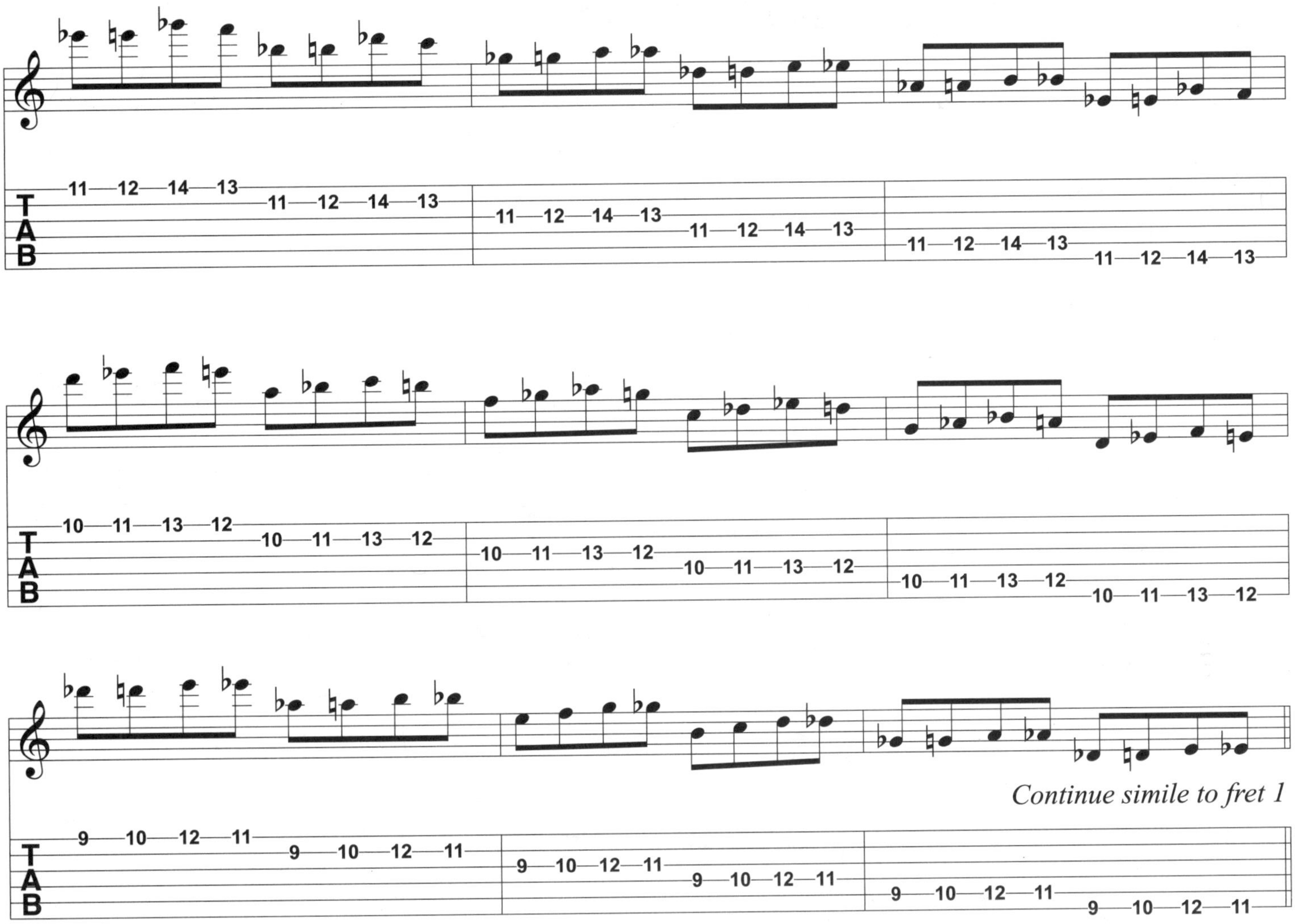

The Most Basic Foundation for Left-Hand Technique: Variations on Exercise 1

There are 23 variations, or 24 total patterns, that can be played from the initial four-note pattern, 1–2–3–4. The numbers represent each finger of the left hand (1 = 1st finger, 2 = 2nd finger, etc.) as well as the frets in 1st position. The combined 24 variations follows:

1–2–3–4	2–1–3–4	3–1–2–4	4–1–2–3
1–2–4–3	2–1–4–3	3–1–4–2	4–1–3–2
1–3–2–4	2–3–1–4	3–2–1–4	4–2–1–3
1–3–4–2	2–3–4–1	3–2–4–1	4–2–3–1
1–4–2–3	2–4–1–3	3–4–2–1	4–3–1–2
1–4–3–2	2–4–3–1	3–4–1–2	4–3–2–1

This seems like an awful lot to tackle in one sitting, so break it up and play one column per day. Try playing column one on Monday, column two on Tuesday, column three on Wednesday, etc. This will help you focus on playing every variation.

This exercise and all its variations are the most basic foundation for left-hand technique. When you can play with each note clearly and cleanly (no buzz or inadvertent damping with either hand), then you may have something. You simply cannot play Exercise 1 and all the variations enough.

The following is essentially the same as Exercise 1, except you go up one fret every time you move to the next string.

Exercise 2–The Spider Variation

Variations

For additional technique building, apply the 24 variations from Exercise 1 to Exercise 2.

Exercise 3 moves up a string, then goes back. The right-hand part is a little more difficult to master here. You can vary this exercise by changing the finger that you jump to on the next string. For example, in the first measure, you can use finger 2 on the 5th string.

Exercise 3–Four-Note Chromatic Variation

Following is another version which uses three-note groupings. Here, each string is self-contained to a single measure.

Exercise 4–Triplet Variations 5

Variations

Apply the following finger combinations to the exercise above:

1–2–3–4–3–2	2–1–3–4–3–1	3–1–2–4–2–1	4–1–2–3–2–1
1–2–4–3–4–2	2–1–4–3–4–1	3–1–4–2–4–1	4–1–3–2–3–1
1–3–2–4–2–3	2–3–1–4–1–3	3–2–1–4–1–2	4–2–1–3–1–2
1–3–4–2–4–3	2–3–4–1–4–3	3–2–4–1–4–1	4–2–3–1–3–2
1–4–2–3–2–4	2–4–1–3–1–4	3–4–1–2–1–4	4–3–1–2–1–3
1–4–3–2–3–4	2–4–3–1–3–4	3–4–2–1–2–4	4–3–2–1–2–3

The following exercise is very effective in addressing the problem of with "fly-away" fingers, which occurs when you have one or more fingers play a note, leaving the remaining fingers dangling straight and away from the fretboard. This usually applies to fingers 3 and 4, with the pinky being particularly susceptible. Review page 4 for a reminder on left-hand position and the position of readiness.

Exercise 5–Opposing Triplet Pattern 6

Variations

Apply the following fingering variations to Exercise 5:

1–2–1	2–1–2	3–1–3	4–1–4
1–3–1	2–3–2	3–2–3	4–2–4
1–4–1	2–4–2	3–4–3	4–3–4

Don't let the $\frac{9}{8}$ time signature in Exercise 6 throw you off. This exercise is really just a slow three using triplets. In other words, think of it as a slow waltz or in $\frac{3}{4}$ time. Set your metronome to about ♩ = 52.

Exercise 6–Chromatic Triplets 7

The following exercise is similiar to the 1–2–3–4 chromatic fingering but with the majority of the notes on individual strings. Take your time to carefully follow the fingerings, and it will make sense. Best of luck.

Exercise 7–Four-Finger Chromatic Cross-String Study 8

Exercise 8 is a three-finger version of the previous exercise. Begin it like Exercise 7, and check the fingerings carefully.

Exercise 8–Three-Finger Chromatic Cross-String Study 9

Shifts

One of the primary skills required to get around on the guitar is *position shifting,* which means being able to accurately move from one position to another. The following shifting exercises are designed to develop control and dexterity. They start the same way as the basic chromatic exercise we've learned, but instead of switching to the next string when the four-note pattern is complete, you shift up the neck on the same string to the next four frets. If you're working on patterns that begin with the 1st finger, you should be on fret 1, followed by fret 5, fret 9, then fret 13.

If you're working on an acoustic guitar and are limited to 12 frets, stop after the second shift with your 1st finger on fret 9. Once you reach your highest desired position, switch to the next string at the same fret and play the pattern moving down the neck in the reverse order (frets 13, 9, 5, and 1).

Note: We usually use ⁄ to indicate slide notes, but in the following, it's used to notate position shifting.

Exercise 9–Single-String Shift 10

Variations

Now, try to apply the 24 variations to Exercise 9. This exercise gets really tricky when you're playing patterns that begin with your 2nd and 3rd fingers, as the shifts are more difficult to keep accurate. Remember that we are aiming for clean. Fast will come.

You might play a variation of Exercise 9 using only your 1st and 4th fingers to focus on the shifts. These two-note exercises can be expanded to include the other combinations of fingers: 1–3, 2–3, 2–4, or 3–4. In those cases, there will be more shifts as you travel up the neck. For example, the 1–3 exercise will shift from the 1st fret to the 4th, then to the 7th, then to the 10th, etc. The combinations of fingers with only one fret between them will travel up the neck one fret at a time.

There are two different ways to play each variation. The first is with all the finger combinations ascending on each string. The second is to play the finger combination ascending up the neck, then when you switch to the next string, play the same combination descending while shifting your hand down the neck. Combining the ascending and descending combinations helps keep things a little more interesting as well as making it a little more musical.

Exercise 10–Two-Note Shift **11**

Another way to break down Exercise 9 further is to work on just the shift. On the 6th string, play the 4th fret A♭ with your 4th finger, then jump to the 5th fret A with your 1st finger. Then jump immediately back to the 4th fret A♭ with your pinky. Repeat this back and forth slowly to get the feel of that shift in your hands. Once you're feeling really confident, try it with your eyes closed.

Exercise 11–Two-Finger String-Shift Only **12**

Another variation to explore is "The Crunch." Here, we use either the 1–3 or 1–4 finger combination, but we play them one fret away from each other, shifting up the neck of the guitar. This is, in a way, the opposite of what we normally try to do—which is to stretch our hand to cover more frets. The following exercises, unlike most left-hand exercises, actually get more difficult as we move up the neck, with the frets getting closer together.

Exercise 12–The Crunch 13

This last variation is "The Snake," named so because of the way it slides back and forth up the neck of the guitar. It's a variation of the basic 1–2–3–4 fingering in Exercise 1.

Start with finger 1, then immediately shift up one fret with that finger. Next, play fingers 2, 3, and 4, then shift up one fret with finger 4, then back down on 3, then 2. Now you should be back at finger 1, but two frets higher up the neck. Repeat this up the neck. There will be two variations written out with several more suggested.

Exercise 13–The Snake with Outside Shift 14

A variation on Exercise 13, Exercise 14 again snakes up the neck, but this time the shifts occur on the inside fingers: fingers 2 and 3.

Exercise 14–The Snake with Inside Shift 15

Variations

There are two additional variations on Exercise 13. The first is the *alternate shift,* or shifting on fingers 1 and 3, then shifting on fingers 2 and 4. There is also the *consecutive shift* variation, where you shift on fingers 1 and 2, then on fingers 3 and 4.

Odd Groupings

On page 7, we learned a single-string exercise (Metronome Exercise 1) that changes in note duration—from quarter notes all the way to thirty-second notes—while using the same metronome setting. Here, that exercise is adapted for adjacent strings. *Odd tuplet groupings* have also been added. These are groups of notes, like triplets, with an odd number of notes, like five or seven per beat. The odd groupings may be difficult at first but are worth the effort to master. They require a certain "letting go" of the time to help keep the timing fluid. Start very slowly at around ♩= 40.

Metronome Exercise 2 16

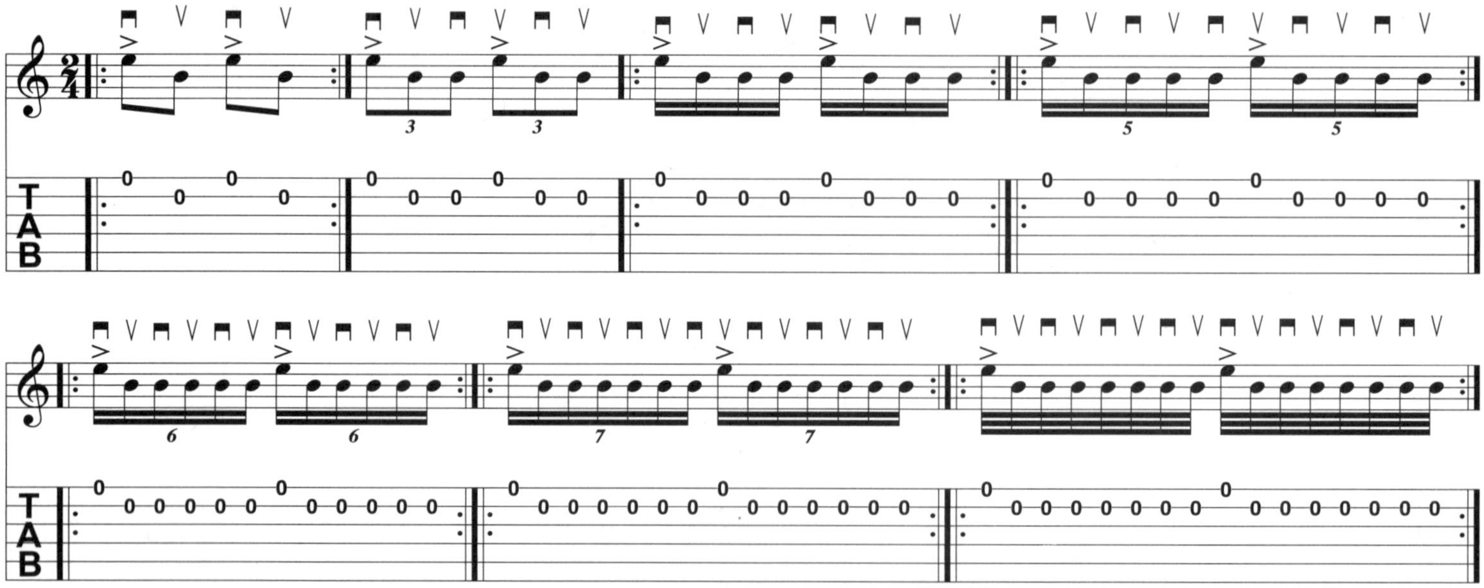

The odd-grouping exercises in this book will be very useful for breaking out of ruts. When done properly, this kind of playing has a soaring quality, allowing you to "float" above the time, not tied to or constricted by it. Think of the playing of guitar legends Jeff Beck and Allan Holdsworth.

The following is a preparatory exercise that will help establish the feel of quintuplets. Make sure the first note on the new string happens right on the click of the metronome. You may use alternate picking with these, but it's not strictly necessary since we're dealing with odd groups of notes. One thing to make sure of is that the notes are evenly spaced over the amount of time allotted for them, which in this case is two beats. Here is where strict alternate picking offers a slight advantage. It's a little harder at first but wins out in the end.

Exercise 15—Chromatic Quintuplet Prepatory Exercise 17

Once the timing of quintuplets is established, move on to the next exercise. In Exercise 16, we'll take the basic left-hand ascending pattern of 1–2–3–4 on each string and descending 4–3–2–1 pattern on each string, and play them in quintuplets. It helps to take some time to feel out each group before you try it in time. You'll notice the first group of five begins on the 1st finger. The second group begins on the 2nd finger; third group, 3rd finger; and fourth group, 4th finger. The fifth group, on the high E string, brings us back to the 1st finger. Now shift up one fret with the 4th finger, and repeat the note we just played. We're now descending from the pinky one fret higher than where we started. The string-change pattern reverses itself (first descending group of quintuplets begins on finger 4, second group on finger 3, etc.). At the bottom, shift on the 1st finger, then repeat the note and ascend another fret higher. Be sure to accent the notes on beats 1 and 3, as this will help keep your time steady. To reverse the exercise and descend the neck, simply shift down one fret at the top and bottom of the exercise, where you would have shifted up in the initial exercise.

Exercise 16–Chromatic Quintuplet Exercise 18

Next is a preparatory exercise for *septuplets,* or groups of seven. It is essentially the same as the quintuplet exercise, but you need to squeeze two more notes in the same amount of time. If you can't, slow down the metronome to get the notes in. Try going back to play the quintuplet exercise again at the slower speed. It's important to be able to sense the difference between the five- and the seven-note feel. They are very different.

Exercise 17–Chromatic Septuplet Preparatory Exercise 19

Next is the four-note-per-string version, with the one-fret shift at the top and the bottom. This time, though, the note at the top is not repeated, while the note at the bottom is.

Exercise 18–Chromatic Septuplet Exercise 20

Following are exercises where you can see how these odd groups can be applied to scales–in this case, the C Major scale. Notice how the septuplet facilitates the seven-note major scale so that the root of the scale falls right on the beat, which does not happen if you're playing straight eighth or sixteenth notes.

Exercise 19–One-Octave C Major Scale with Quintuplets 21

Exercise 20–Extended One-Octave C Major Scale with Quintuplets 22

Exercise 21–Two-Octave C Major Scale with Quintuplets

Exercise 22–Two-Octave C Major Scale with Quintuplets (Alternate Fingering)

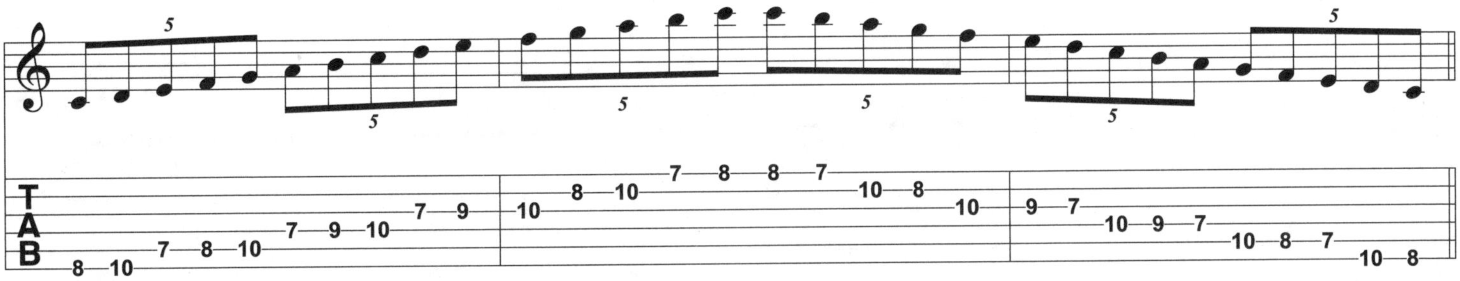

Exercise 23–Two-Octave C Major Scale with Septuplets

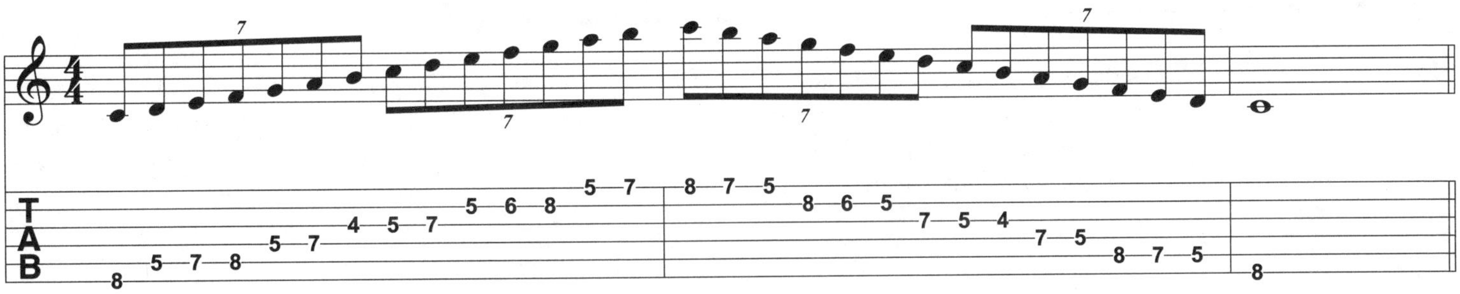

Exercise 24–Two-Octave C Major Scale with Septuplets (Alternate Fingering)

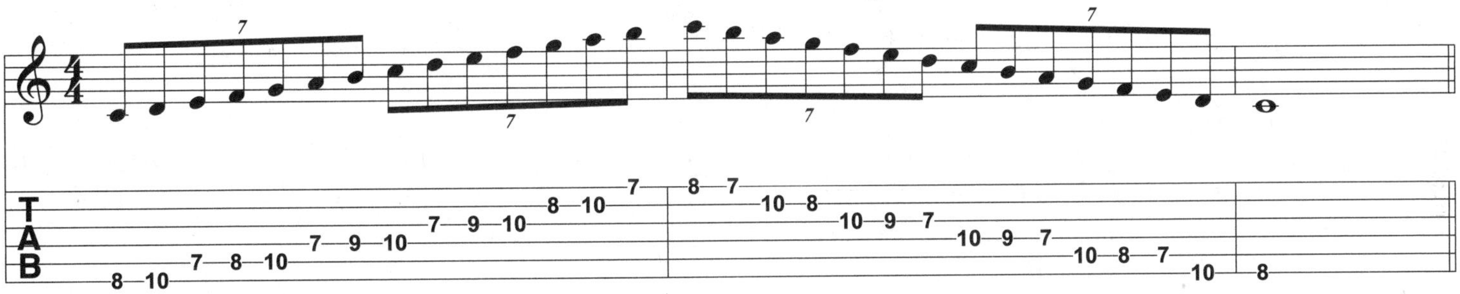

Exercise 25–C Major Chord-Tone Exercise

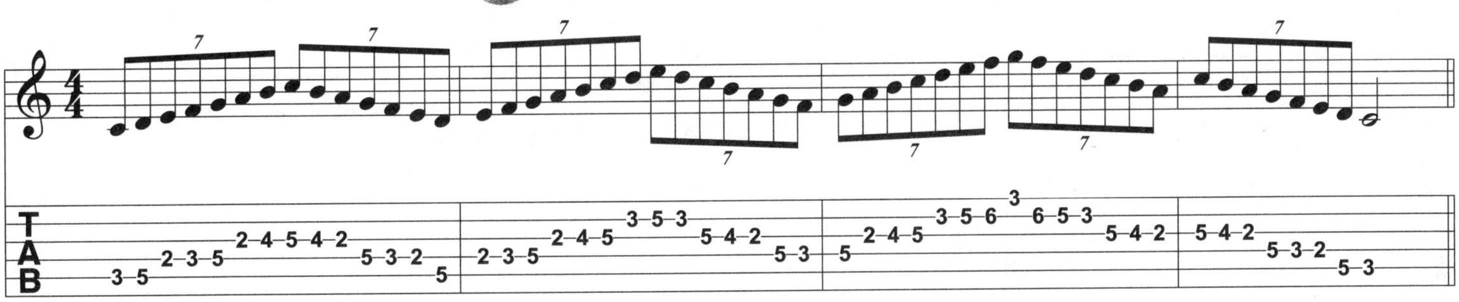

Make It Musical

28

This is a passage in C Major using septuplets as a motif.

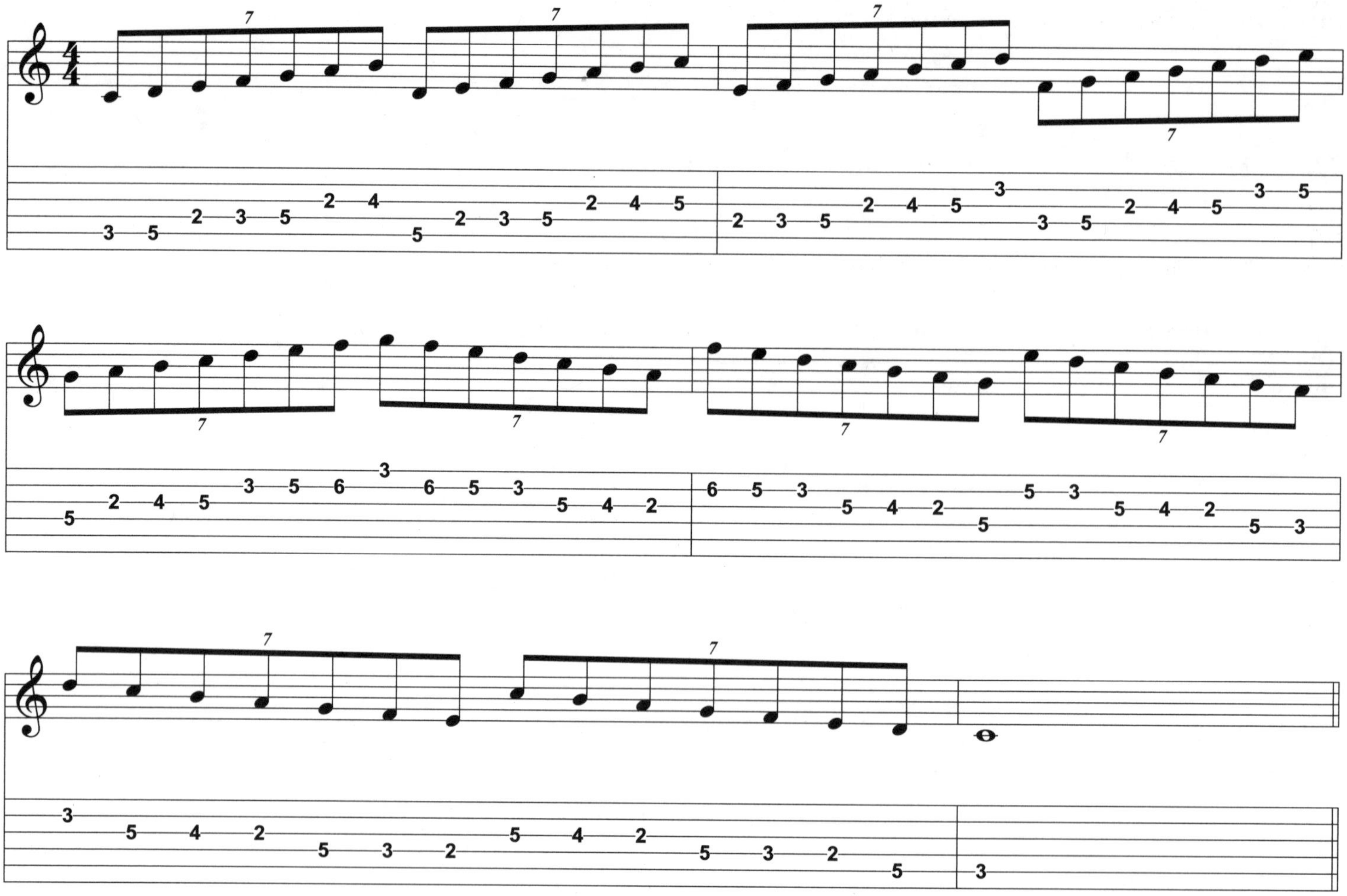

TWO-STRING EXERCISES

The next series of exercises involve phrases that jump strings. This is where things get a little more challenging, and it is also where the principle of simultaneous release becomes very important—it organizes the fingers of the left hand so that they are consistent in the way they apply and release pressure. Using it, your brain will be free to concentrate on what comes next, not how to get there. Apply this principle daily to make your left-hand playing much more effective and efficient.

Exercise 26—Two-String Study (Open) 29

Here is the same exercise with no open strings.

Exercise 27–Two-String Exercise (Closed) 30

Here, we'll continue Exercise 27, but reverse the notes on the top string in each measure.

Exercise 28–Variation in $\frac{3}{4}$ 31

Exercise 29 and its variations are excellent for practicing the principle of simultaneous release. Begin slowly and pay particular attention to when the fingers leave the fretboard. In the first measure, even though we are changing strings on the "and" of beat 1, leave the 1st finger on the 2nd string. On beat 2, place the 3rd finger and leave the 1st and 2nd fingers where they are. On the "and" of beat 2, place the 4th finger and leave the other three fingers, so that at the end of the first measure all four fingers are down. Note that though only the 4th finger is actually applying pressure to play a note, it doesn't have to work very hard as it's getting help from the 2nd finger behind it. This is how this concept applies to efficiency with the left hand. Now, release all the fingers at the same time to begin the next measure.

Exercise 29–Chromatic Pairs 32

Exercise 30–Crossing Melodic Lines 33

Exercise 31–Extended Crossing Melodic Lines 34

Make It Musical

Here's an intervallic line in the style of Jimmy Herring. 35

This is a rather bizarre line in the style of King Crimson. Watch out for the slides in measure 6. Left-hand fingerings are included for this one. Best of luck! 36

DOUBLE STOPS AND THE BARRE

Double stops, playing two notes at once, present special challenges. Moving two fingers simultaneously requires twice the accuracy and focus. Acquiring dexterity with double stops encourages the use of all your fingers—instead of always having to slide the same two fingers up and down the neck, especially when playing 5ths, or *power chords.* Later in this chapter, we will work on the *barre,* or placing a left-hand finger to fret multiple strings at the same time.

Exercise 32—Double Stops on Consecutive Strings 37

Exercise 33—Single-Note Variation 38

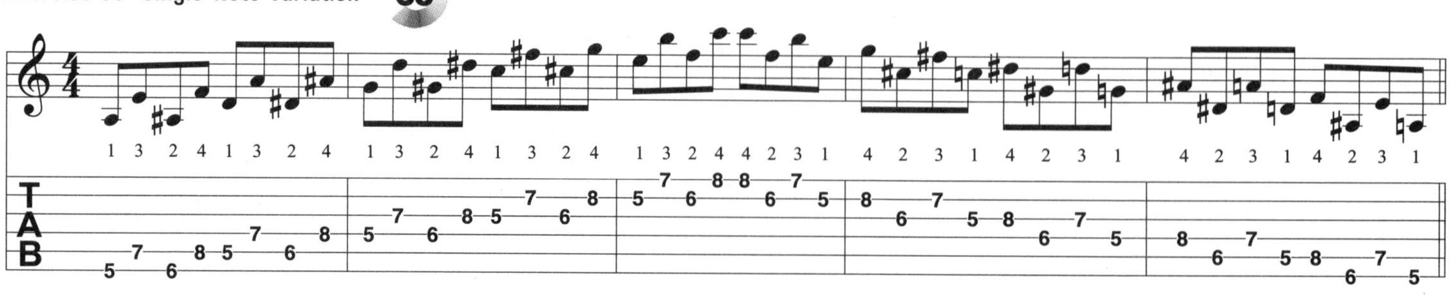

Apply each of the variations below to the exercises on the previous page. These are different intervals requiring different finger combinations. You will find some to be much more musical than others, but being able to play them all is important, as we're aiming for independence with all the different combinations of pairs of fingers.

Exercise 34–Double-Stop Variations

In exercise 35, keep the finger combinations on a single pair of strings to shift them up and down the neck.

Exercise 35–Double-Stop Combinations with Shifts

All the double-stop combinations in Exercise 34 can be applied in this manner: Play the first two double stops, then shift four frets higher on the same two strings instead of changing to different strings. Continue up the neck as far as your instrument will allow.

Exercise 36–Walking Pairs 40

Barre

The barre is a very important part of left-hand development. Being able to barre from two to six strings with any finger is important, particularly the first two fingers. The following exercise will help develop the strength necessary to do this. Remember to keep the left hand in front of the neck in order to employ the larger muscles of the hand along with the muscles in the fingers. Keeping the fingers straight will help make sure all the strings sound clearly.

Exercise 37–Barre Study 41

Here's our old friend, the power chord. This exercise employs a two-string barre along with a fretted note.

Exercise 38–Power-Chord Prepatory Exercise 42

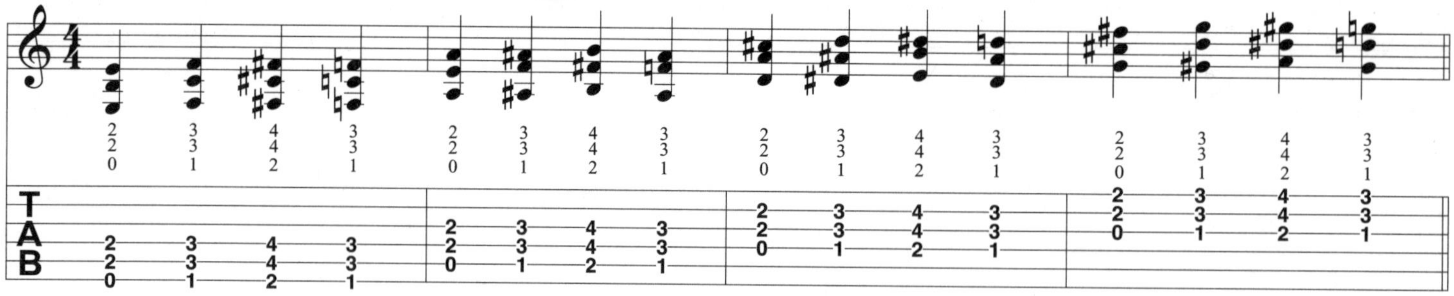

Exercise 39–Power-Chord Exercise with Shifts 43

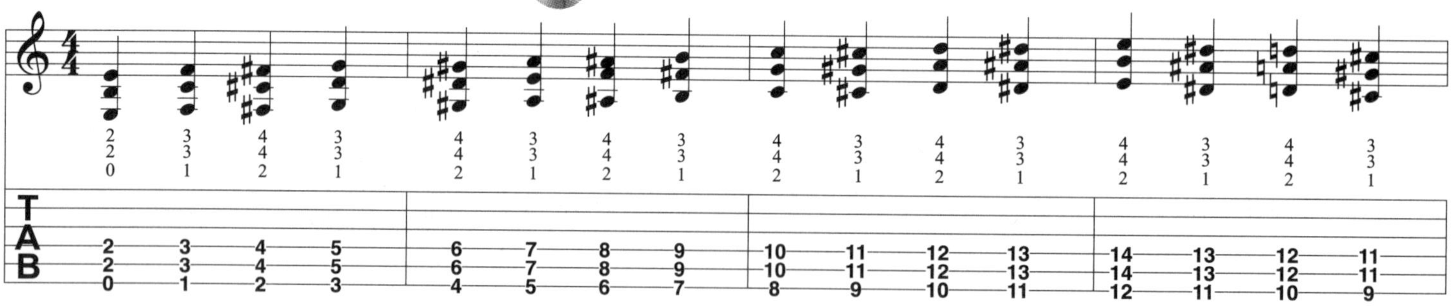

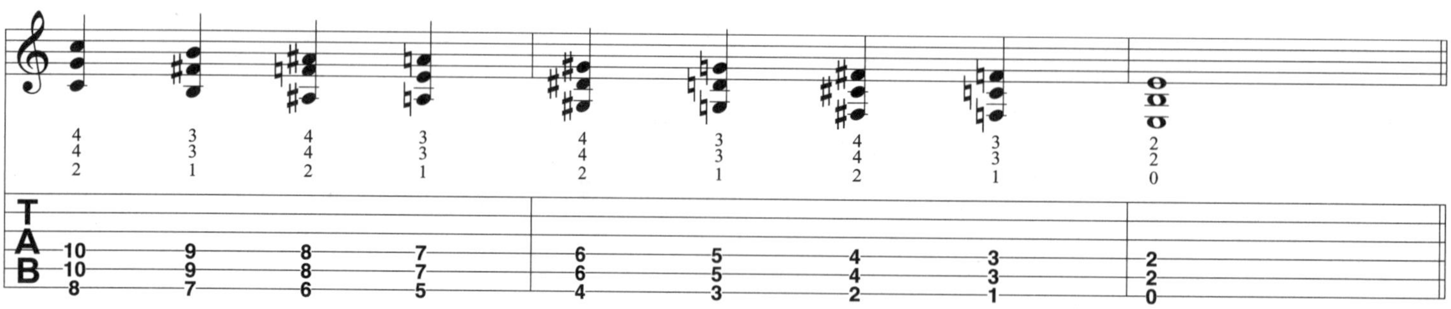

Play Exercise 39 using string combinations 5–4–3, 4–3–2, and 3–2–1. This will reinforce being able to play power chords using different finger combinations instead of being locked into a single method of movement, namely sliding the 1st and 3rd fingers around the neck. This makes for a much cleaner transition between chords.

In the following exercise, barre all six strings at the 1st fret, then play the other three notes with normal fingering.

Exercise 40–Chromatic Barre Exercise 44

Make It Musical

In the following exercises, we will be applying the small barre to triad scales moving up the neck of the guitar.

E Major Triad Scale 45

E Major Triad Scale (Alternate Fingering) 46

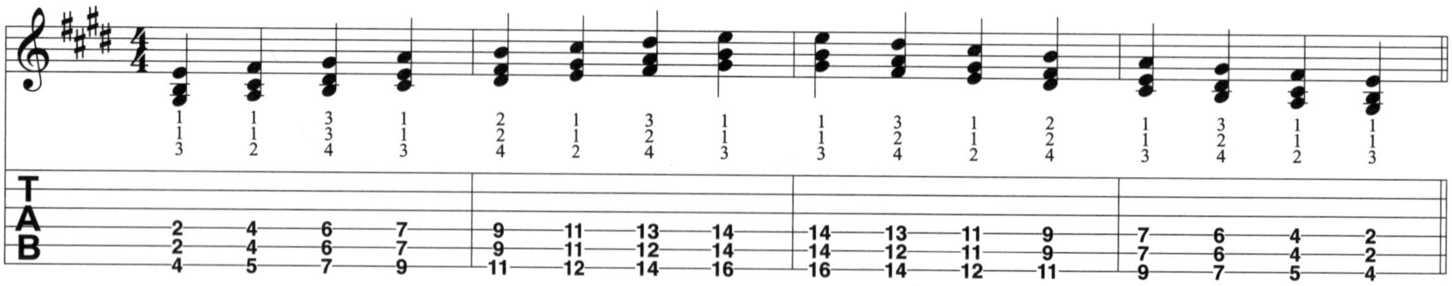

E Major Triad Scale (Alternate Octave) 47

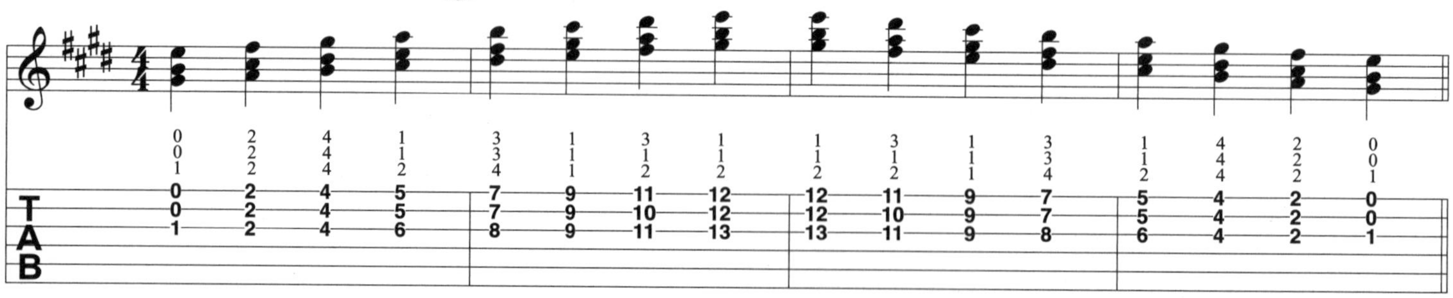

Triad Ending 48

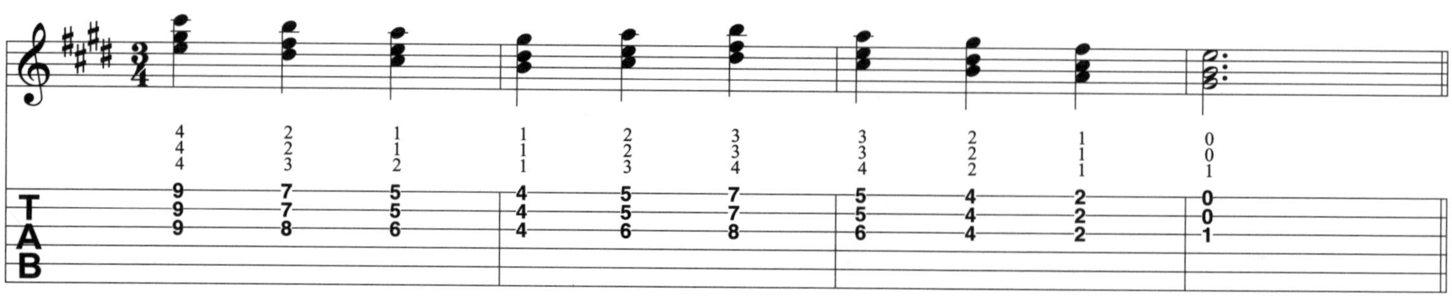

SLURRED NOTES

An important left-hand technique is the *slur.* This refers to notes that are played but not picked, and it is accomplished on the guitar with techniques such as *hammer-ons* and *pull-offs.* Ascending notes are played with hammer-ons, while descending notes are played with pull-offs. With hammer-ons, you pick a note then quickly fret a higher note to sound it. Use a little extra force in order for the string to continue to vibrate. Pull-offs are accomplished by fretting and picking an upper note, then pulling downward to cause a lower note that is already fretted to sound. With practice, you will be able to hammer-on and pull-off multiple notes in a row, as well as on multiple strings at a time.

H = Hammer-on
P = Pull-off

Exercise 41–Hammer-On Single-String Combinations

49

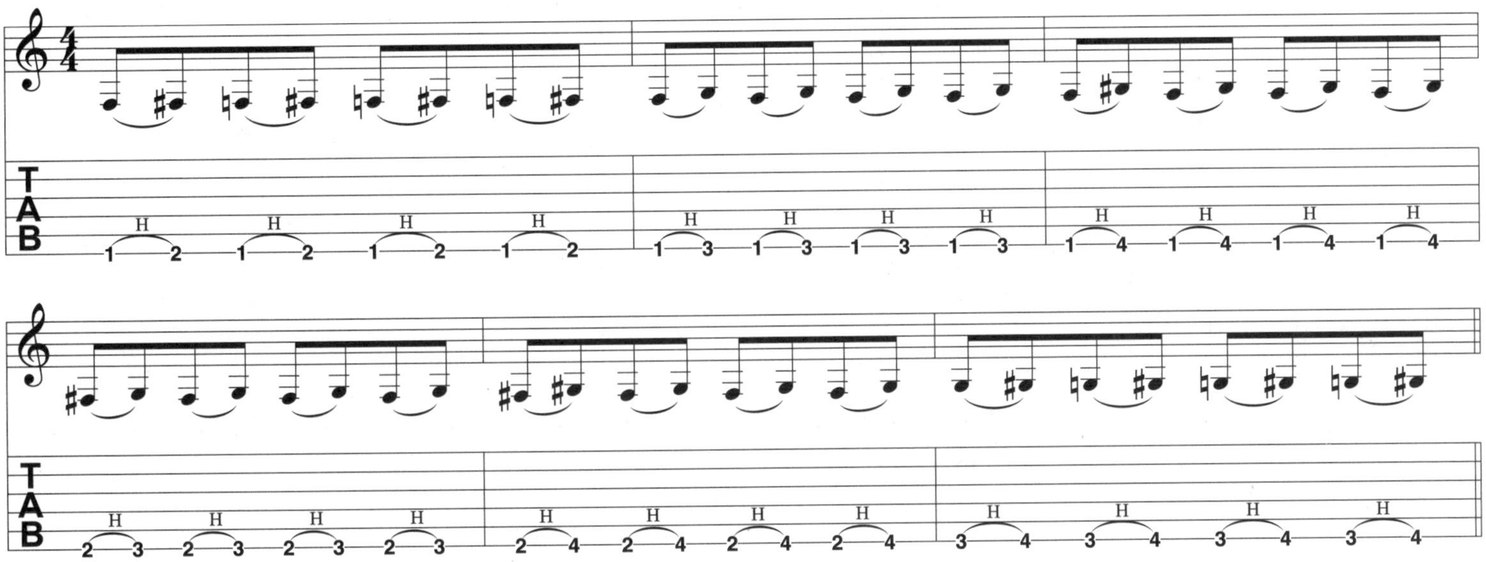

Repeat the hammer-on combinations in Exercise 41 on the rest of the strings.

Exercise 42–Hammer-On Each String Combinations

50

Repeat Exercise 42 with each finger combination.

Exercise 43–Hammer-On Open-String Exercise 51

In Exercise 43, we played open-string hammer-ons on the 6th string using all four left-hand fingers. Now, play it on the rest of the strings.

Exercise 44–Pull-Off Single-String Combinations 52

We played pull-offs using different finger combinations on the 6th string in Exercise 44. Continue on, and play it on the rest of the strings.

Exercise 45–Pull-Off Each String Combinations 53

Exercise 45 featured pull-offs on each string using the same finger combination. Now, repeat with each finger combination.

Exercise 46–Pull-Off Open-String Exercise 54

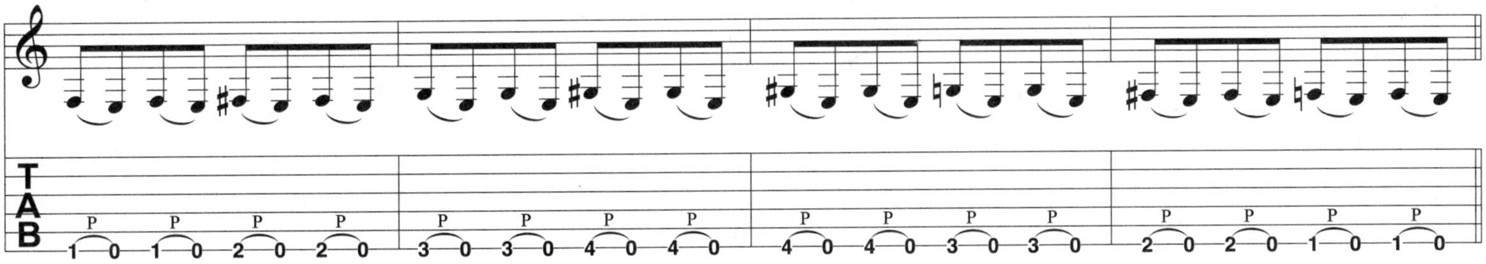

We just played pull-offs to the open 6th string. Now do the same on the rest of the strings.

Exercise 47–Hammer-On/Pull-Off Combination 55

The exercise above is a combination of a hammer-on followed by a pull-off, using triplets. Only the first note in the triplet is picked. Repeat with each finger combination: 1–2–1, 1–3–1, 1–4–1, 2–3–2, 2–4–2, 3–4–3.

Exercise 48–Pull-Off/Hammer-On Combination 56

We just played a pull-off followed by a hammer-on. Again repeat with each finger combination: 2–1–2, 3–1–3, 4–1–4, 3–2–3, 4–2–4, 3–4–3.

Here is the hammer-on/pull-off combination ascending followed by the opposite combination descending, all on a single string. Play on each string.

Exercise 49–Single-String Hammer-On/Pull-Off Combination 57

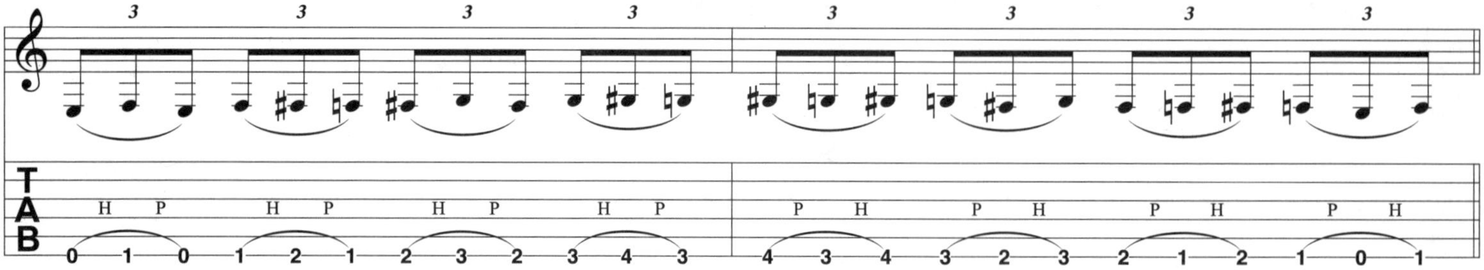

Exercise 50 hammers two notes in a row. Pay particular attention to the second hammer-on, making sure the note is clearly heard.

Exercise 50–Three-Note Hammer-On Exercise 58

The following exercise pulls-off two notes, the opposite of Exercise 50. Again, make sure the second pull-off is clearly heard.

Exercise 51–Three-Note Pull-Off Exercise 59

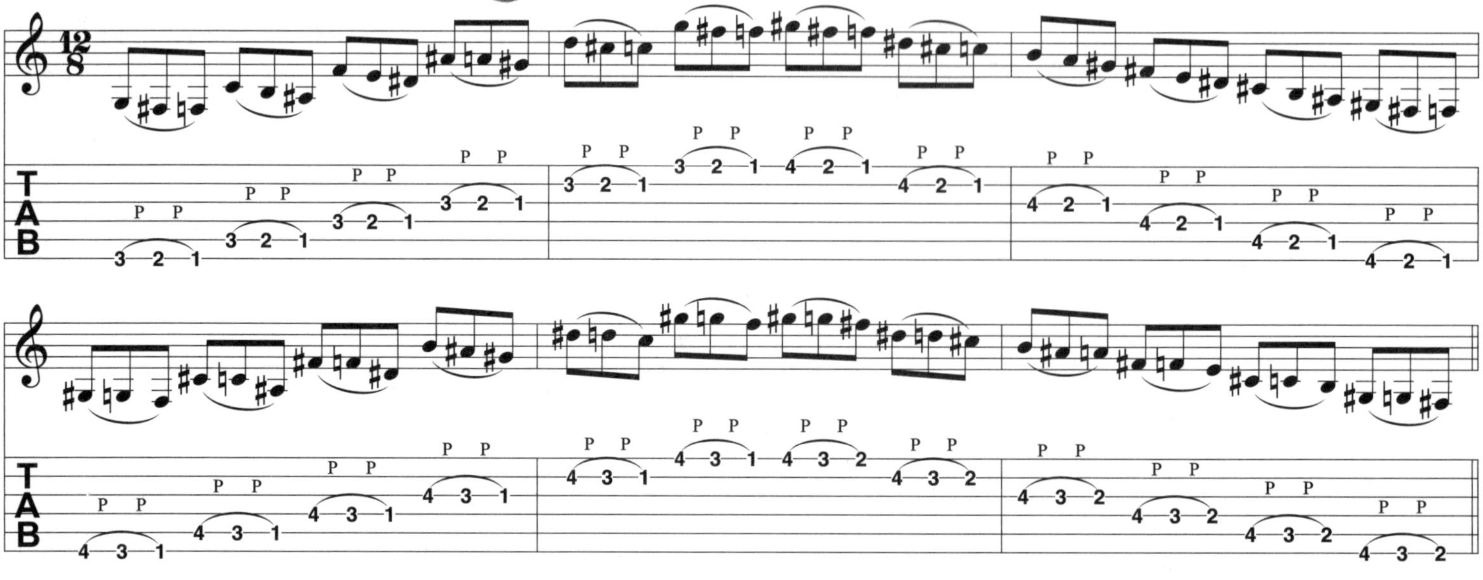

The hammer-on/pull-off combination in Exercise 52 efficiently gets us five notes with only one stroke of the pick.

Exercise 52–Three-Note Pull-Off/Hammer-On Exercise 60

Exercise 53–Four-Note Hammer-On/Pull-Off Exercise 61

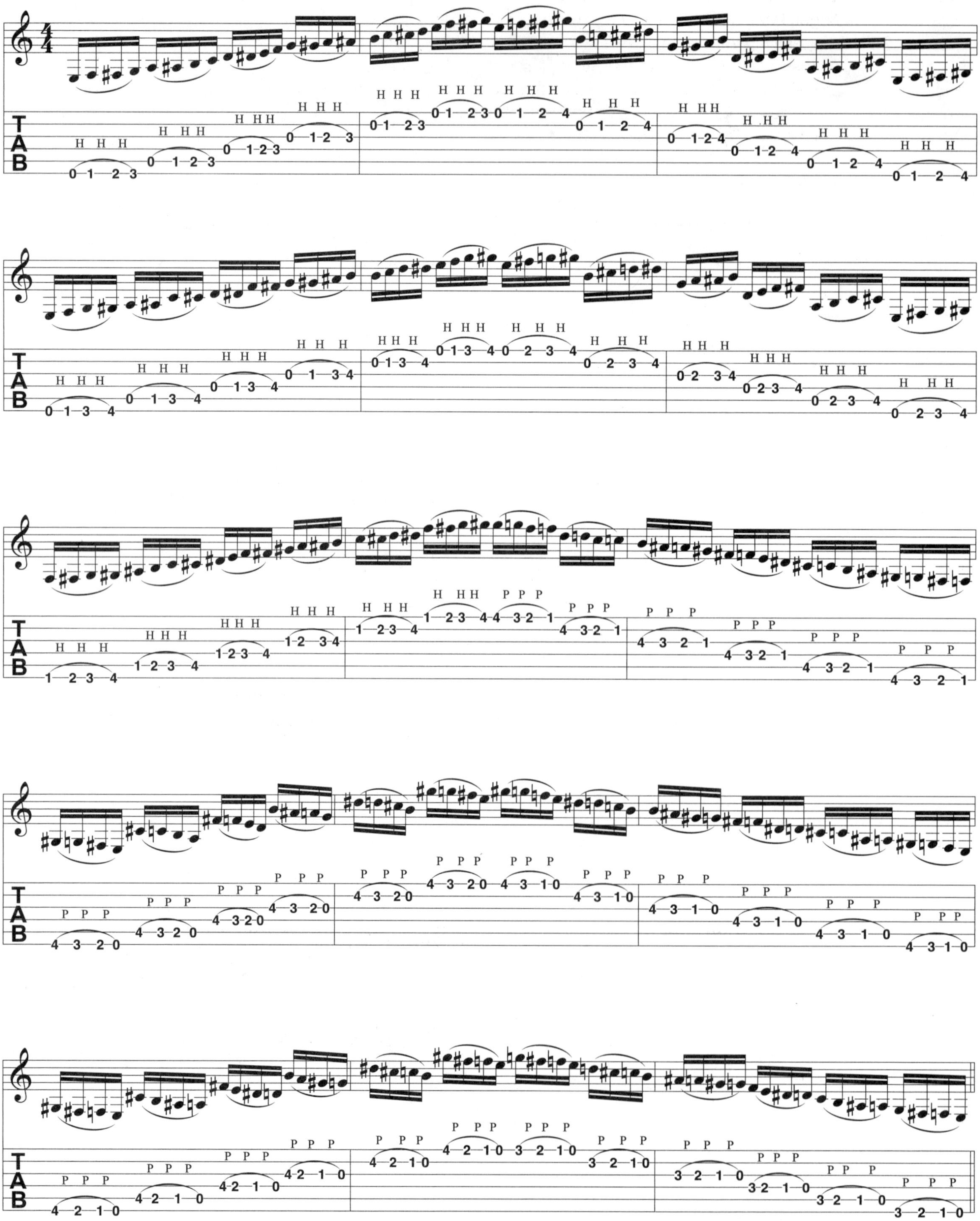

Exercise 54 employs hammer-ons and pull-offs, and incorporates a *finger roll,* which is a left-hand technique that allows you to move smoothly and effortlessly from one string to the next using the same finger. For instance, take a look at measure 1 of Exercise 54. We'll see a finger roll with the 2nd finger, where it doesn't ever really lose contact with the neck of the guitar, but instead, releases pressure and "rolls" over to the adjacent string. You may find turning your finger slightly to the side helps make this technique smoother. The trick is to not have the finger pull off the string you're leaving. If you are able to release the pressure of your finger without losing contact with the string, the transition will be smooth and silent.

Exercise 54–Finger-Roll Exercise 62

Make It Musical

The following piece features hammer-ons and pull-offs to play a twangy little musical line up and down on the G-string. Fingerings are included for this one, but you could just as easily incorporate your 4th finger on the higher notes to make it a little more stationary. The piece may be tricky at first, especially when you're playing it slowly, but take your time and pay attention to the slurs, and you'll have it under your fingers in no time.

63

STRETCH EXERCISES

Stretching, in this case, refers to the practice of stretching the tendons and muscles of the hand in order to help facillitate reaching and playing farther on the guitar neck. Generally, all the exercises presented so far have spanned four frets, one for each finger. Even when they involve shifts of position, there were still four frets that fell under your fingers. The point of the exercises in this chapter is to be able to reach at least six frets with the left hand. It is possible to reach much farther, just watch Allan Holdsworth, but those extremes are really outside the scope of this book and conventional playing.

Careful Practice

It is quite possible to hurt yourself while doing some of these stretching exercises. *It is very important to move slowly and to stop immediately if you feel pain.* A certain amount of discomfort is to be expected, but that is very different from pain. Practice these exercises only after you have thoroughly warmed up, but even then, try not to stretch for more than 15–20 minutes a day. We all want to get better, but listen to your body, and when it tells you to stop doing something, take heed. Be careful with hand-exercise gadgets, as they can lead you to believe you are warm and stretched when in fact you are not. In addition, stretches performed with your other hand (on the floor, for instance) may feel good and certainly do no harm, but if you want to be a better guitar player, it is better to stretch whille holding a guitar.

Two Steps Forward, One Step Back

The exercises in this chapter are situated to begin farther up the neck, as the frets are closer together there. So, many of these exercises get more difficult as you get closer to the nut. Once you have the pattern under your fingers, feel free to adjust the exercise if it is too difficult where it is. After you're playing it comfortably for a week or so, move the exercise toward the nut by two frets. Try it there for a while. If it's too difficult after a day or two to play smoothly and cleanly, or if you cannot keep your fingers planted (remember the principle of simultaneous release), move it back up the neck by one fret. The exercise will be easier, and you will have gotten one fret farther in your progress. This method is similar to the one we employed with the metronome: two steps forward and one step back, which is still one step of forward progress.

Exercise 55 puts a two-fret gap in between fingers 1 and 2, plus note the alternative fingerings. Fingers 2 and 3 are where you need to be particularly careful when stretching. Turning your hand toward the nut will help with that stretch, as will placing the fingers so that they are making contact with the string to the left of the pad.

Exercise 55–Four-Note Chromatic Stretch 1 64

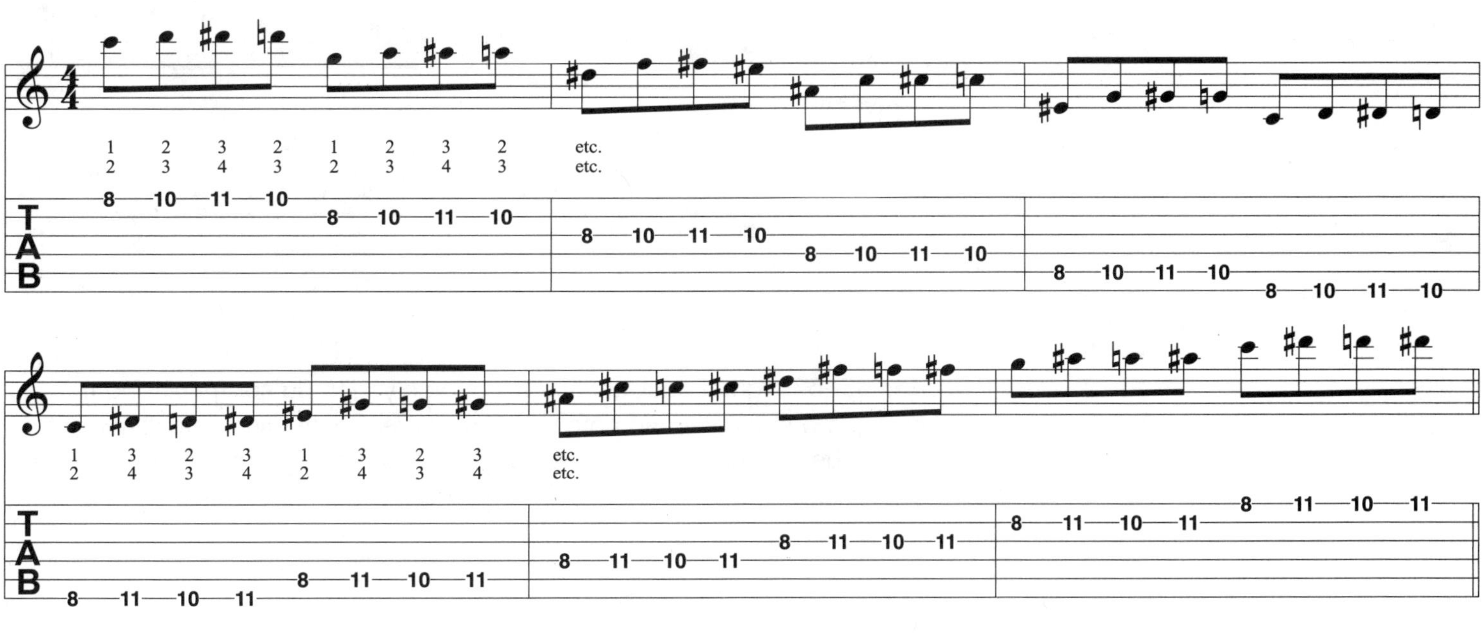

We put that two-fret gap right where you feel it in Exercise 56. Again, be careful not to hurt yourself. The alternate fingering might be easier here.

Exercise 56–Four-Note Chromatic Stretch 2 65

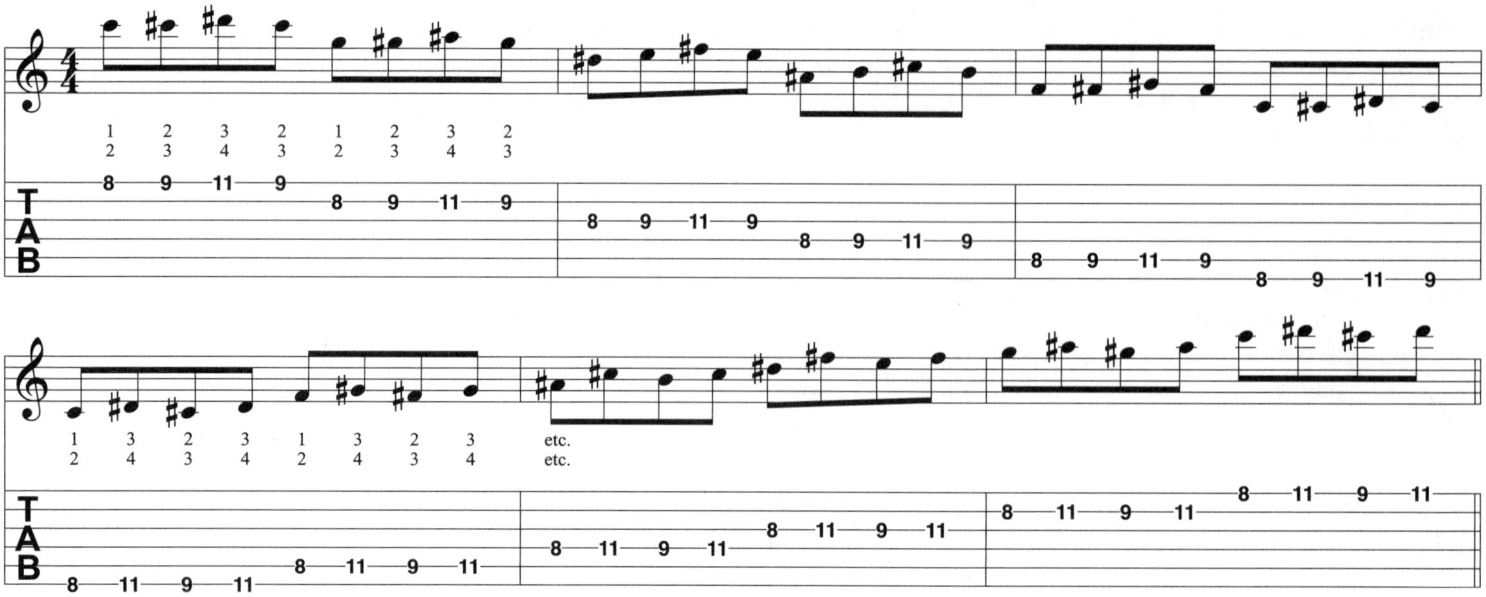

In Exercise 57, there is a two-fret gap between each of the frets in the pattern. Make sure to practice the alternative fingering as it is important to be able to use either your 2nd or 3rd fingers in this pattern. You will see why in the next exercises.

Exercise 57–Four-Note Chromatic Stretch 3 66

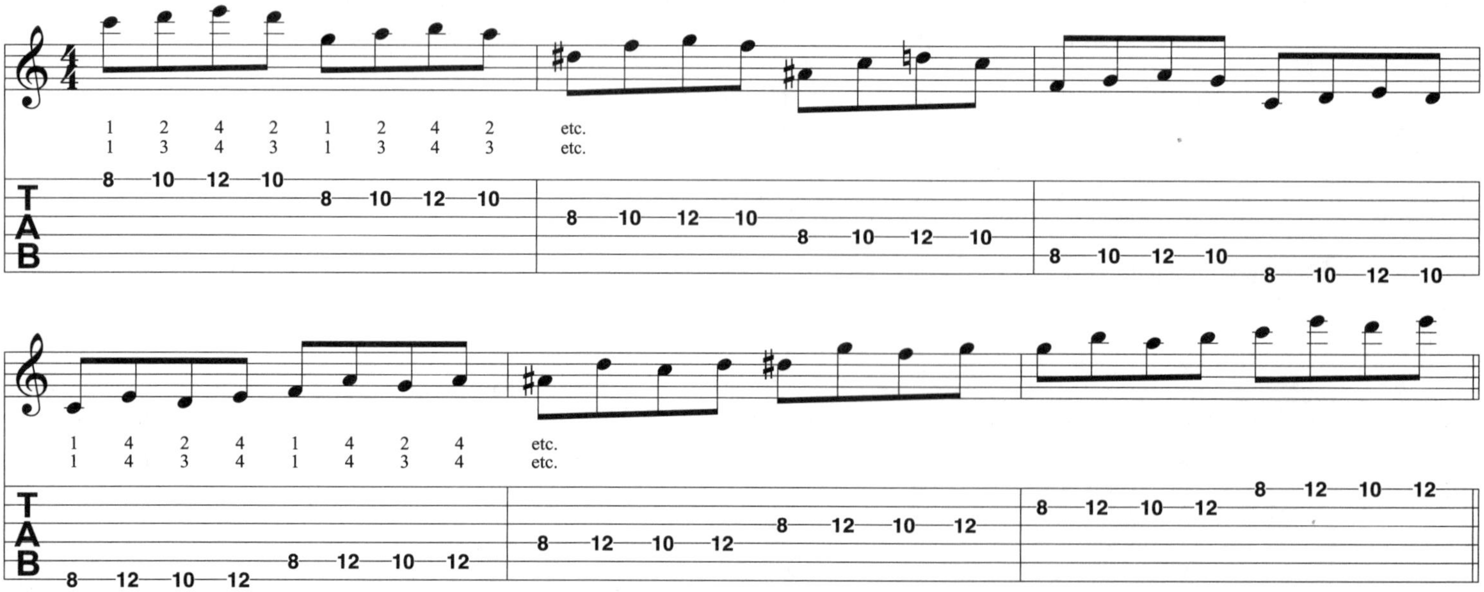

Variations

You can vary Exercises 55–57 a great deal, and we encourage you to do so. Try playing the four-note pattern beginning with the second note in the measure. So, the fingering variation for the exercise above would be 2–4–2–1, with a one-fret gap between each note. Then, it will be 4–2–1–2. Apply these variations to the preceeding three exercises.

Exercise 58 features a one-octave C Major scale starting on each of your left-hand fingers, which will require different stretches for each fingering. Note that there are several different positions involved here.

Exercise 58–One-Octave C Major Scale Stretch Fingering 67

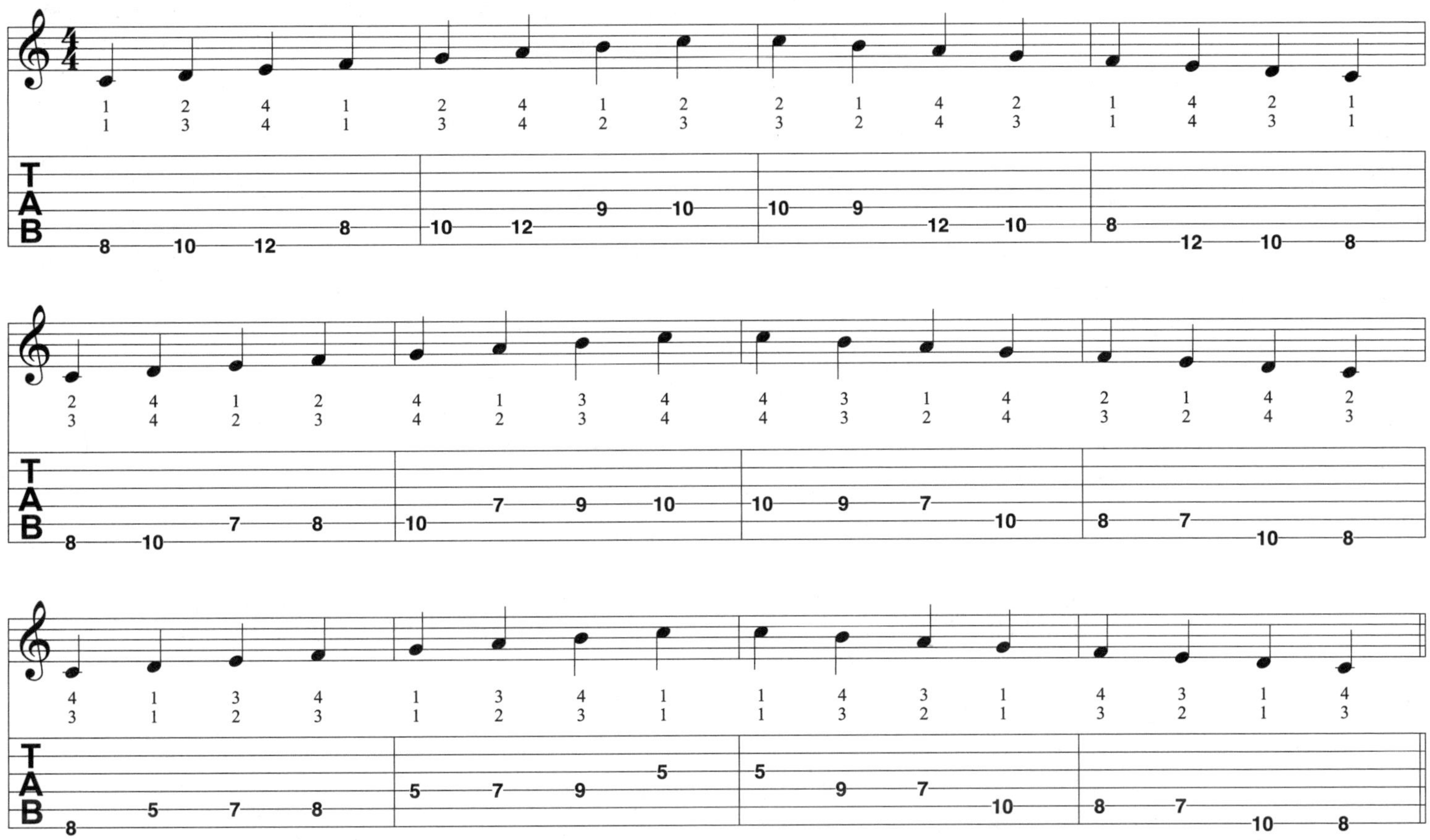

Exercise 59 begins with the 1st finger in the 8th position.

Exercise 59–Two-Octave C Major Scale Stretch Fingering 1 68

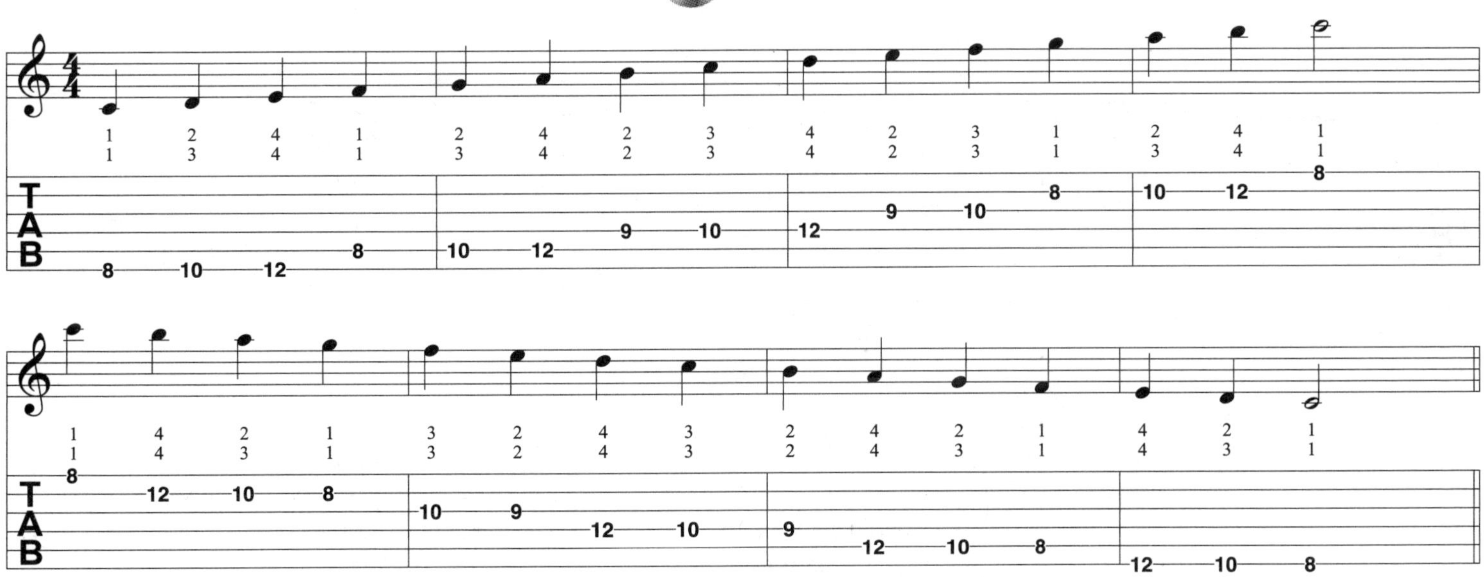

Here, we begin with the 2nd and 3rd fingers in 7th position.

Exercise 60–Two-Octave C Major Scale Stretch Fingering 2

69

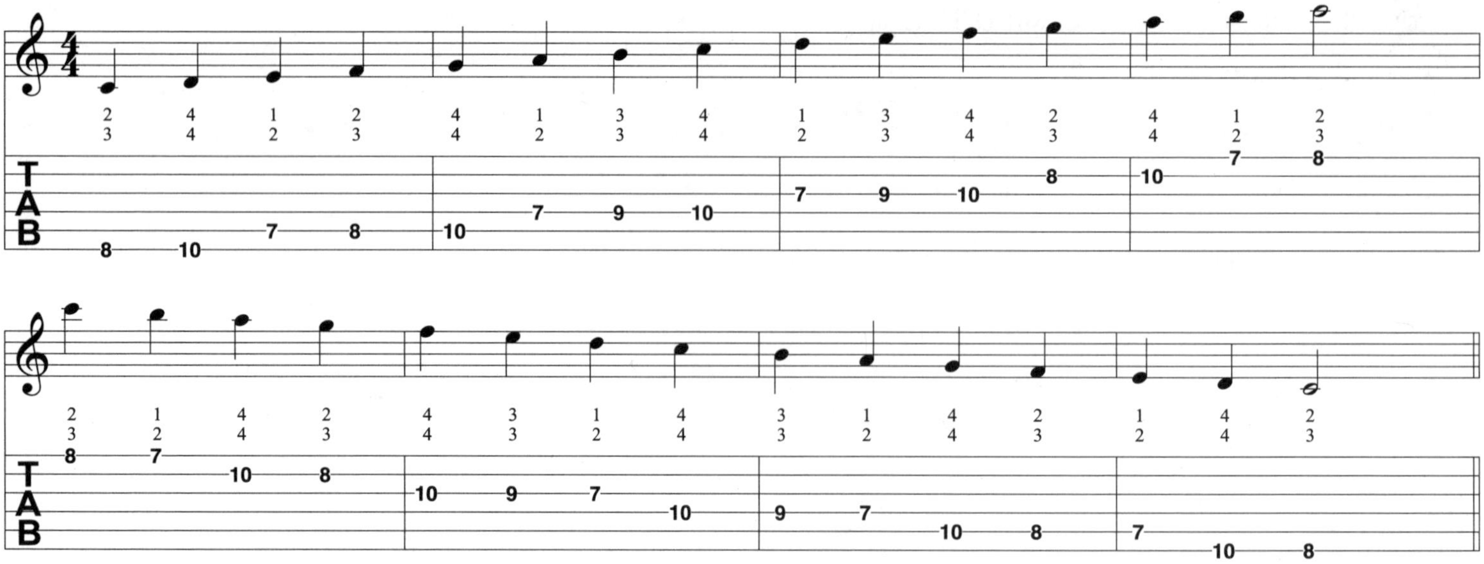

Exercise 61 begins in the 5th position with the 4th finger at the 8th fret.

Exercise 61–Two-Octave C Major Scale Stretch Fingering 3

70

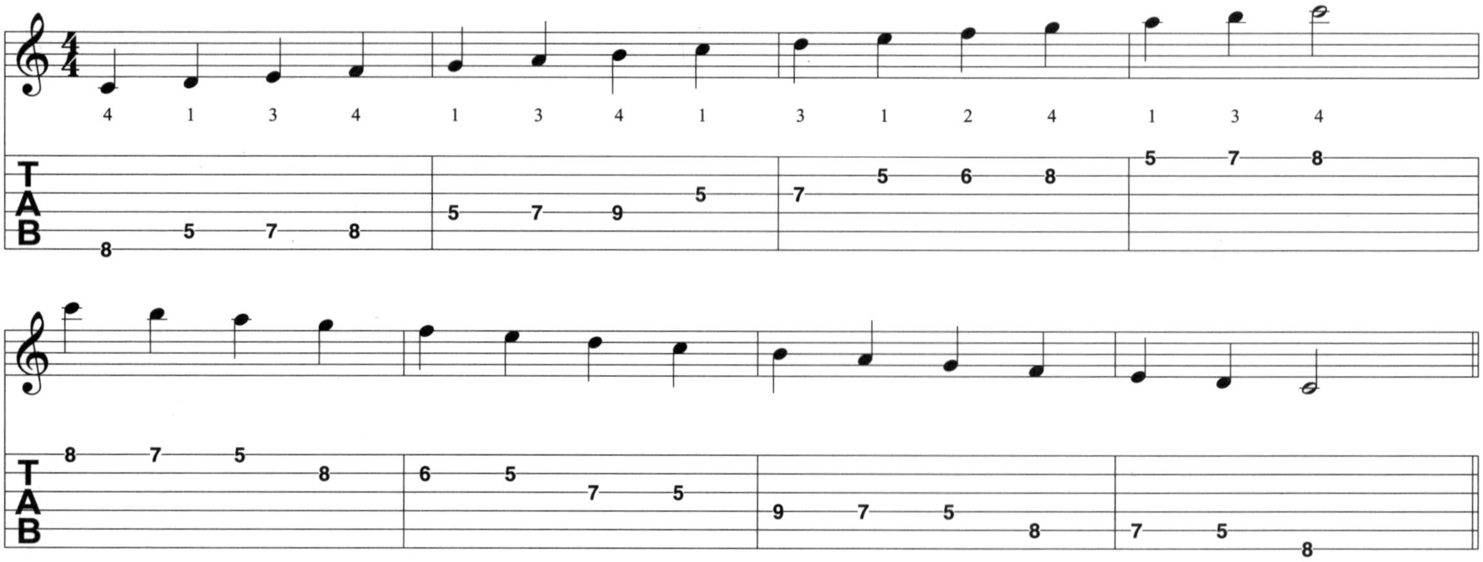

Exercise 62 involve shifting the fingers up and down by one fret. Remember to keep your fingers planted once they are placed.

Exercise 62–Chromatic Stretch 71

Play Exercise 63 as if you are playing a chord, meaning all four notes should sound at once. It focuses on the inside four strings but can be played on any of the four string groups. Play it down the neck as far as you can.

Exercise 63–Single-Fret Chord Crawl 72

Exercise 64 is essentially the same exercise as Exercise 63 but with two-fret shift. Watch out for that third measure.

Exercise 64–Double-Fret Chord Crawl 73

The foundation for Exercise 65 was introduced in Chapter 1 as Exercise 7. Here it is again with a one-fret gap between the notes. The third and fourth fingering variations are particularly challenging. Play each fingering variation all the way through the entire exercise before moving on to the next one.

Exercise 65–Cross-String Chromatic (Extended Fingering) 74

Make It Musical

It's time again to apply these exercises to a musical situation. Here's a stretchy line inspired by Andy Summers of The Police.

75

ODDS AND ENDS

The following exercises are all in C Major. They may not all start on C but are nonetheless in C. Exercise 66 employs the open string as a pedal tone, then moves up the neck on each string. In those places where there is a one-fret gap between notes, feel free to vary the fingering by using either your 2nd or 3rd finger. It would be advantageous, however, to be able to use either. Exercise 66 is written out so that the highest note is on the 17th fret. If you can't reach that, play it as high as you can on the neck of your instrument. Have fun with this one.

Exercise 66–Diatonic Single-String Prepatory Exercise 76

A complete version of the exercise (with all the pattern and finger combination variations) is presented on the following pages. Once you have played it on the 6th string, move on to the 5th string, using only the notes in C Major, beginning in 1st position. Finally, play the exercise on the remaining strings.

Exercise 67–Diatonic Single-String Exercise 77

Exercise 68 is an oddball exercise that's sort of a musical tongue-twister. It will help develop finger independence vertically over multiple strings. It's uses the 1–3 and 2–4 finger combinations on the left hand, but you could easily vary it with a 1–2 and 3–4 combination, or 1–4 and 2–3.

Exercise 68–Vertical Pairs Exercise 78

MUSICAL PIECES

The following short pieces are based on popular songs and incorporate the concepts and techniques introduced in this book. Seeing examples of how these ideas are used will hopefully give you some insight into how to incorporate them into your own music.

In the Style of "Long Distance Runaround" by Yes 79

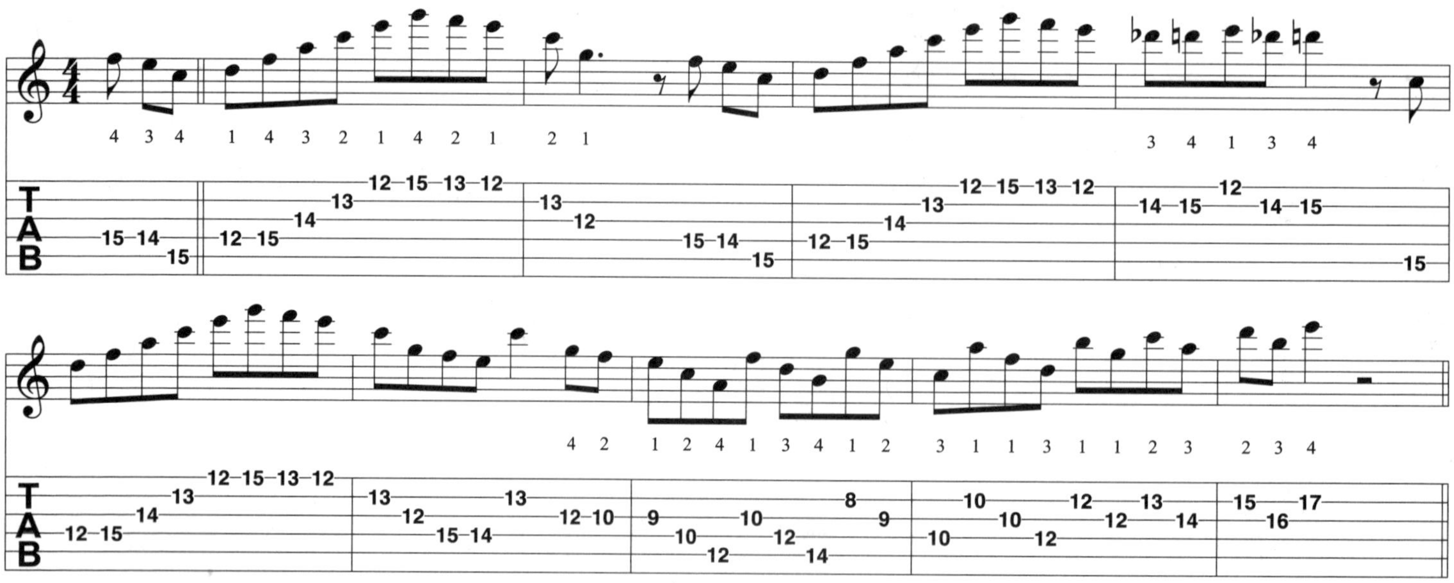

In the Style of "La Villa Strangiato" by Rush 80

In the Style of "Black Dog" by Led Zeppelin

81

In the Style of "Larks' Tongues in Aspic, Part III" by King Crimson 82

TAB

In the Style of "Message in a Bottle" by The Police 83

Final Thoughts

We hope you have gotten something useful out of this book. We covered as much standard left-hand technique as we could for now–techniques like hybrid picking and two-hand tapping were intentionally left out as they fall into a somewhat different category.

The musical pieces at the end of the book represent ways to employ many of the techniques presented. Work consistently, cultivate good habits, and you will make tremendous progress in a relatively short period of time. As always, the ultimate goal is to become a better musician.

Good luck and have fun.